To:

_____

From:

_____

Date:

_____

PROMISES & PRAYERS

for Teachers

FC
FAMILY
CHRISTIAN
PRESS

PROMISES & PRAYERS

for Teachers

ISBN 1-58334-145-5

The quoted ideas expressed in this book (but not scripture verses) are not, in all cases, exact quotations, as some have been edited for clarity and brevity. In all cases, the author has attempted to maintain the speaker's original intent. In some cases, quoted material for this book was obtained from secondary sources, primarily print media. While every effort was made to ensure the accuracy of these sources, the accuracy cannot be guaranteed. For additions, deletions, corrections or clarifications in future editions of this text, please write FAMILY CHRISTIAN PRESS.

Certain elements of this text, including quotations, stories, and selected groupings of Bible verses, have appeared, in part or in whole, in publications produced by Brighton Books of Nashville, TN; these excerpts are used with permission.

Printed in the United States of America
Cover Design & Page Layout: *Bart Dawson*

For Teachers Everywhere

Table of Contents

>>
INTRODUCTION
>>

*H*enry Adams correctly observed, "A teacher affects eternity; he can never tell where his influence stops." And, those words have never been more true than they are today. We live in a difficult, fast-paced, temptation-filled world; more than ever, our young people need the direction and the leadership provided by teachers who know and love God.

On the pages that follow, we consider topics of interest to Christians who teach. Each brief chapter contains Bible verses, a quotation from a noted thinker, and a prayer. This text provides helpful reminders for the everyday challenges that face today's teachers. Whether you teach graduate school or Sunday School, whether you lecture at seminary or at Vacation Bible School, you need and deserve a regularly scheduled conference with the ultimate Teacher. After all, you are God's emissary, a person charged with molding lives—a truly awesome responsibility. God takes your teaching duties very seriously, and so should you.

So, if you are fortunate enough to find yourself in the role of teacher, accept a hearty congratulations and a profound word of thanks. And then, take a few moments to consider the promises and prayers on these pages. Remember that God honors your profession just as surely as He offers His loving abundance to you and your students. With God's help, you are destined to reshape eternity. It's a big job, but don't worry; together, you and God can handle it.

I will instruct you and teach you
in the way you should go;
I will counsel you and
watch over you.

—

Psalm 32:8 NIV

ABUNDANCE

I am come that they might have life, and that they might have it more abundantly.

—John 10:10 KJV

But this I say, He which soweth sparingly shall reap also sparingly; and he which soweth bountifully shall reap also bountifully.

—2 Corinthians 9:6 KJV

My cup runneth over. Surely goodness and mercy shall follow me all the days of my life: and I will dwell in the house of the LORD for ever.

—Psalm 23:5-6 KJV

Ask and it will be given to you; seek and you will find; knock and the door will be opened to you. For everyone who asks receives; he who seeks finds; and to him who knocks, the door will be opened.

—Matthew 7:7-8 NIV

His master replied, "Well done, good and faithful servant! You have been faithful with a few things; I will put you in charge of many things. Come and share your master's happiness!"

—Matthew 25:21 NIV

*T*he words of John 10:10 remind us that Jesus offers the abundant life to all who believe in Him. Today, let us accept God's promise of spiritual abundance. And then, in a spirit of optimism and faith, let us share our abundance with all who cross our paths, especially our students.

God loves you and wants you to experience peace and life—abundant and eternal.

—Billy Graham

—A Prayer—

*T*hank You Father for the abundant life that is mine through Christ Jesus. Guide me according to Your will, and help me to be a worthy teacher through all that I say and do. Give me courage, Lord, to claim the rewards You have promised, and when I do, let all the glory be Yours.

—Amen

ADVERSITY

Be of good cheer; I have overcome the world.
—John 16:33 KJV

No discipline seems pleasant at the time, but painful. Later on, however, it produces a harvest of righteousness and peace for those who have been trained by it.
—Hebrews 12:11 NIV

For though a righteous man falls seven times, he rises again....
—Proverbs 24:16 NIV

The Lord lifts the burdens of those bent beneath their loads. The Lord loves the righteous.
—Psalm 146:8 NLT

Come to me, all you who are weary and burdened, and I will give you rest. Take my yoke upon you and learn from me, for I am gentle and humble in heart, and you will find rest for your souls. For my yoke is easy and my burden is light.
—Matthew 11:28-30 NIV

From time to time, teachers and students alike face adversity, discouragement, or disappointment. But, whatever our circumstances, God stands ready to protect us...if we let Him. Psalm 147 promises, "He heals the brokenhearted, and binds their wounds" (v. 3). When we are troubled, we must call upon God, and then, in His own time and according to His own plan, He will heal us.

God allows us to experience the low points of life in order to teach us lessons that we could learn in no other way.

—*C. S. Lewis*

—A PRAYER—

Heavenly Father, You are my strength and refuge. I can face the difficulties of this day because You are with me. You are my light and pathway. As I follow You, Father, I can overcome adversity just as Jesus overcame this world.

—*Amen*

ANGER

And the servant of the Lord must not strive; but be gentle unto all men, apt to teach, patient; in meekness instructing those that oppose themselves....

—2 Timothy 2:24-25 KJV

Let all bitterness, and wrath, and anger, and clamor, and evil speaking, be put away from you, with all malice: and be ye kind one to another, tender-hearted, forgiving one another, even as God for Christ's sake hath forgiven you.

—Ephesians 4:31-32 KJV

But I tell you that men will have to give account on the day of judgment for every careless word they have spoken. For by your words you will be acquitted, and by your words you will be condemned.

—Matthew 12:36-37 NIV

But I tell you that anyone who is angry with his brother is subject to judgment.

—Matthew 5:22 NIV

As every teacher knows, the task of educating is not without its frustrations. But, God does not intend that anger should rule our lives. Far from it. He intends that we turn away from anger whenever possible and forgive our neighbors just as we seek forgiveness for ourselves. So, when you are tempted to lose your temper over the minor inconveniences of life, don't. Whether you are inside the classroom or out, turn away from anger, hatred, bitterness, and regret. That we should be forgiving is not just God's commandment, it is the only truly decent way to live.

Anger is the noise of the soul; the unseen irritant of the heart; the relentless invader of silence.

—*Max Lucado*

—A PRAYER—

Lord…sometimes, it is so easy to lose my temper and my perspective. When anger burdens my soul, enable me to calm myself and to be a witness to Your truth and righteousness. Let my students see me as a model of kindness and forgiveness, today and every day.

—*Amen*

ASKING GOD

Verily, verily, I say unto you, He that believeth on me, the works that I do shall he do also; and greater works than these shall he do; because I go unto my Father. And whatsoever ye shall ask in my name, that will I do, that the Father may be glorified in the Son. If ye shall ask any thing in my name, I will do it.

—John 14:12-14 KJV

And I say unto you, Ask, and it shall be given you; seek, and ye shall find; knock, and it shall be opened unto you. For every one that asketh receiveth; and he that seeketh findeth; and to him that knocketh it shall be opened. If a son shall ask bread of any of you that is a father, will he give him a stone? or if he ask a fish, will he for a fish give him a serpent? Or if he shall ask an egg, will he offer him a scorpion? If ye then, being evil, know how to give good gifts unto your children; how much more shall your heavenly Father give the Holy Spirit to them that ask him?

—Luke 11:9-13 KJV

You do not have, because you do not ask God.

—James 4:2 NIV

*A*re you in need? Ask God to sustain you. Are you troubled? Take your worries to Him in prayer. Are you weary? Seek God's strength. In all things great and small—inside the classroom and outside it—seek the healing power of God's grace. He hears your prayers, and He will answer.

God insists that we ask, not because He needs to know our situation, but because we need the spiritual discipline of asking.

—*Catherine Marshall*

—A PRAYER—

*D*ear Lord, You are the giver of all things good. When I am in need, let me come to You in prayer. You know the desires of my heart, Lord; grant them, I ask. Yet not my will, Father, but Your will be done.

—*Amen*

>>

ATTITUDE

>>

For the word of God is living and active. Sharper than any double-edged sword, it penetrates even to dividing soul and spirit, joints and marrow; it judges the thoughts and attitudes of the heart.

—Hebrews 4:12 NIV

Therefore, since Christ suffered in his body, arm yourselves also with the same attitude, because he who has suffered in his body is done with sin. As a result, he does not live the rest of his earthly life for evil human desires, but rather for the will of God.

—1 Peter 4:1-2 NIV

Your attitude should be the same as that of Christ Jesus: Who, being in very nature God, did not consider equality with God something to be grasped, but made himself nothing, taking the very nature of a servant, being made in human likeness. And being found in appearance as a man, he humbled himself and became obedient to death—even death on a cross!

—Philippians 2:5-8 NIV

A teacher's attitude affects the mood of the entire classroom. If a teacher is upbeat, enthusiastic, and inspired, many students will become enthused. If, however, a teacher is lethargic or bored, students, too, will lose interest. The most memorable teachers—and the ones who do the most for their students—are the teachers who become excited about the subjects they teach…and about life.

A child's formative years are the most important for instilling the right attitudes.

—John Maxwell

—A Prayer—

D ear Lord, let me live my life and teach my students with a spirit of optimism and hope. Whatever circumstances I face, whether good or bad, triumphal or tragic, may my response reflect a God-honoring, Christlike attitude of faith and love for You.

—Amen

BEHAVIOR

Be thou an example of the believers, in word, in conversation, in charity, in spirit, in faith, in purity.

—1 Timothy 4:12 KJV

Therefore, brethren, stand fast, and hold the traditions which ye have been taught, whether by word, or our epistle.

—2 Thessalonians 2:15 KJV

You shall walk in all the way which the Lord your God has commanded you, that you may live, and that it may be well with you, and that you may prolong your days in the land which you will possess.

—Deuteronomy 5:33 NASB

He will teach us of his ways, and we will walk in his paths.

—Isaiah 2:3 KJV

Who among you is wise and understanding? Let him show by his good behavior his deeds in the gentleness of wisdom.

—James 3:13 NASB

*T*eachers serve as powerful examples to their students. Wise teachers understand that while words often fall upon closed ears, actions do not. And, godly teachers behave accordingly.

If we have the true love of God in our hearts, we will show it in our lives. We will not have to go up and down the earth proclaiming it. We will show it in everything we say or do.

—D. L. Moody

—A Prayer—

*L*ord, I pray that my actions will always be consistent with my beliefs. I know that my deeds speak more loudly than my words. May every step that I take reflect Your truth and love, and may my students be drawn to You because of my words and my deeds.

—Amen

THE BIBLE

Every word of God is pure: he is a shield unto them that put their trust in him.

—*Proverbs 30:5 KJV*

Blessed are those who hunger and thirst for righteousness, for they will be filled.

—*Matthew 5:6 NIV*

For the word of God is quick, and powerful, and sharper than any two-edged sword, piercing even to the dividing asunder of soul and spirit, and of the joints and marrow, and is a discerner of the thoughts and intents of the heart.

—*Hebrews 4:12 KJV*

Jesus answered and said unto him, If a man love me, he will keep my words: and my Father will love him, and we will come unto him, and make our abode with him.

—*John 14:23 KJV*

Heaven and earth will pass away, but my words will never pass away.

—*Matthew 24:35 NIV*

God has given us the Holy Bible for the purpose of knowing His commandments, His wisdom, His love, and His Son. When we study God's teachings and apply them to our lives, we live by the Word that shall never pass away.

❦

The vigor of our spiritual lives will be in exact proportion to the place held by the Bible in our lives and in our thoughts.

—*George Müller*

—A Prayer—

Dear Lord, the Bible is Your gift to me; let me use it. When I stray from Your Holy Word, Lord, I suffer. But, when I place Your Word at the very center of my life, I am blessed. Make me a faithful student of Your Word so that I might be a faithful teacher in Your world, this day and every day.

—*Amen*

CELEBRATION

David and the whole house of Israel were celebrating with all their might before the LORD, with songs and with harps, lyres, tambourines, sistrums and cymbals.

—2 Samuel 6:5 NIV

At the dedication of the wall of Jerusalem, the Levites were sought out from where they lived and were brought to Jerusalem to celebrate joyfully the dedication with songs of thanksgiving and with the music of cymbals, harps and lyres.

—Nehemiah 12:27 NIV

Shout for joy to the LORD, all the earth. Worship the LORD with gladness; come before him with joyful songs.

—Psalm 100:1-2 NIV

So now we can rejoice in our wonderful new relationship with God—all because of what our Lord Jesus Christ has done for us in making us friends of God.

—Romans 5:11 NLT

The 118th Psalm reminds us that today, like every other day, is a cause for celebration. God gives us this day; He fills it to the brim with possibilities, and He challenges us to use it for His purposes. Today is a non-renewable resource—once it's gone, it's gone forever. Our responsibility—as Christians and as teachers—is to use this day in the service of God's will as we share His wisdom and His love.

This is the day the LORD has made; let us rejoice and be glad in it.

—King David

—A Prayer—

Lord, You have placed countless people along my path: let me celebrate their lives and encourage them. Today, let me share a smile and a kind word with all my students and all whom I meet. And, let the love of Your Son Jesus be reflected in my care and concern for others, this day and every day.

—Amen

CHARACTER

The man of integrity walks securely, but he who takes crooked paths will be found out.

—Proverbs 10:9 NIV

A good name is more desirable than great riches; to be esteemed is better than silver or gold.

—Proverbs 22:1 NIV

...in all things showing yourself to be a pattern of good works; in doctrine showing integrity, reverence, incorruptibility....

—Titus 2:7 NKJV

As in water face reflects face, so the heart of man reflects man.

—Proverbs 27:19 NASB

Not only so, but we also rejoice in our sufferings, because we know that suffering produces perseverance; perseverance, character; and character, hope.

—Romans 5:3-4 NIV

Wise teachers understand the importance of character…and teach it. Character is built slowly over a lifetime. It is the sum of every right decision, every honest word, every noble thought, and every heartfelt prayer. It is forged on the anvil of honorable work and polished by the twin virtues of generosity and humility. Character is a precious thing—difficult to build but easy to tear down; godly teachers value it and protect it at all costs…and they encourage their students to do the same.

Character is higher than intellect.

—*Ralph Waldo Emerson*

—A Prayer—

Lord…You are my Father in Heaven. You search my heart and know me far better than I know myself. May I be Your worthy servant, and may I live and teach according to Your commandments. Let me be a person of integrity, Lord, and let my words and deeds be a testimony to You, today and always.

—*Amen*

CHEERFULNESS

A cheerful heart is good medicine....

—Proverbs 17:22 NIV

The cheerful heart has a continual feast.

—Proverbs 15:15 NIV

A cheerful look brings joy to the heart, and good news gives health to the bones.

—Proverbs 15:30 NIV

God loves a cheerful giver.

—2 Corinthians 9:7 NIV

This is the day the LORD has made; let us rejoice and be glad in it.

—Psalm 118:24 NIV

*O*swald Chambers correctly observed, "Joy is the great note all throughout the Bible." He might have added that joy should also be the cornerstone of learning. Today, let us celebrate life as God intended. Today, let us put smiles on our faces, kind words on our lips, and songs in our hearts. And, while we're at it, let's infuse as much joy as we can into the classroom. God loves a cheerful giver *and* a cheerful teacher.

Wondrous is the strength of cheerfulness.

—*Thomas Carlyle*

—A Prayer—

*D*ear Lord, You have given me so many reasons to celebrate. Today, let me choose an attitude of cheerfulness. Let me be a joyful teacher, Lord, quick to smile and slow to anger. And, let me share Your goodness with all whom I meet so that Your love might shine in me and through me.

—*Amen*

CHILDREN

Then there arose a reasoning among them, which of them should be greatest. And Jesus, perceiving the thought of their heart, took a child, and set him by him, and said unto them, Whosoever shall receive this child in my name receiveth me; and whosoever shall receive me, receiveth him that sent me: for he that is least among you all, the same shall be great.

—Luke 9:46-48 KJV

Even a child is known by his actions, by whether his conduct is pure and right.

—Proverbs 20:11 NIV

Train a child in the way he should go, and when he is old he will not turn from it.

—Proverbs 22:6 NIV

Suffer the little children to come unto me, and forbid them not; for of such is the kingdom of God. Verily I say unto you, Whosoever shall not receive the kingdom of God as a little child, he shall not enter therein. And he took them up in his arms, put his hands upon them, and blessed them.

—Mark 10:14-16 KJV

Every child is different, but every child is similar in this respect: he or she is a priceless gift from the Father above. And, with the Father's gift comes immense responsibility for parents and teachers alike. Even on those difficult days when the classroom is in an uproar and the papers are piled to the ceiling, wise teachers never forget the overriding goal of their profession: shaping young minds. The very best teachers shape those minds with love, with discipline, and with God.

When Jesus put the little child in the midst of His disciples, He did not tell the little child to become like His disciples; He told the disciples to become like the little child.

—*Ruth Bell Graham*

—A Prayer—

Lord, You have given me a wonderful responsibility: that of educating my students. Let me teach them, care for them, nurture them, and direct them to You. When I am weary, give me strength. When I am frustrated, give me patience. And, let my words and deeds always demonstrate the love that I feel for them...and for You.

—*Amen*

CHRIST

Therefore if any man be in Christ, he is a new creature: old things are passed away; behold, all things are become new.

—2 Corinthians 5:17 KJV

The next day John seeth Jesus coming unto him, and saith, Behold the Lamb of God, which taketh away the sin of the world.

—John 1:29 KJV

I am the Vine, you are the branches. When you're joined with me and I with you, the relation intimate and organic, the harvest is sure to be abundant.

—John 15:5 MSG

To this end was I born, and for this cause came I into the world, that I should bear witness unto the truth.

—John 18:37 KJV

For the Son of man is come to save that which was lost.

—Matthew 18:11 KJV

Thomas Brooks spoke for believers of every generation when he observed, "Christ is the sun, and all the watches of our lives should be set by the dial of his motion." Christ, indeed, is the ultimate Savior of mankind and the personal Savior of those who believe in Him. As his servants, we should place Him at the very center of our lives. And, every day that God gives us breath, we should share Christ's love and His message with a world that needs both.

I have a great need for Christ; I have a great Christ for my need.

—C. H. Spurgeon

—A Prayer—

Thank You, Lord, for Your Son. His love is boundless, infinite, and eternal. Today, let me pause and reflect upon Christ's love for me, and let me share that love with all my students. And, as an expression of my love for Him, let me share Christ's saving message with a world that desperately needs His grace.

—Amen

CHRIST'S LOVE

As the Father hath loved me, so have I loved you; continue ye in my love.

—John 15:9 KJV

This is my commandment, That ye love one another, as I have loved you. Greater love hath no man than this, that a man lay down his life for his friends.

—John 15:12-13 KJV

Who shall separate us from the love of Christ? shall tribulation, or distress, or persecution, or famine, or nakedness, or peril, or sword?…Nay, in all these things we are more than conquerors through him that loved us.

—Romans 8:35,37 KJV

Jesus Christ the same yesterday, and today, and for ever.

—Hebrews 13:8 KJV

*E*ven though we are imperfect and fallible, even though we have fallen far short of God's commandments, Christ loves us still. His love is perfect and steadfast; it does not waver. May we accept Christ's love, and may we encourage others to do likewise as they welcome Him into their hearts. In today's troubled world, we all need the love and the peace that are found through Jesus.

This hard place in which you perhaps find yourself is the very place in which God is giving you opportunity to look only to Him, to spend time in prayer, and to learn long-suffering, gentleness, meekness—in short, to learn the depths of the love that Christ Himself has poured out on all of us.

—*Elisabeth Elliot*

—A PRAYER—

*D*ear Lord, thank You for the gift of Your Son Jesus, my personal Savior. Let me be a worthy servant of Christ, and let me be ever grateful for His love. Father, You loved me before I was ever born, and You will love me throughout eternity. In return, let me offer my life to You so that I might live according to Your commandments and according to Your plan. Let me always praise You, Lord, as I give thanks for Your Son Jesus and for Your everlasting love.

—*Amen*

CONSCIENCE

So I strive always to keep my conscience clear before God and man.

—Acts 24:16 NIV

Let us draw near to God with a sincere heart in full assurance of faith, having our hearts sprinkled to cleanse us from a guilty conscience and having our bodies washed with pure water.

—Hebrews 10:22 NIV

I will maintain my righteousness and never let go of it; my conscience will not reproach me as long as I live.

—Job 27:6 NIV

Do not conform any longer to the pattern of this world, but be transformed by the renewing of your mind. Then you will be able to test and approve what God's will is—his good, pleasing and perfect will.

—Romans 12:2 NIV

Create in me a pure heart, O God, and renew a steadfast spirit within me.

—Psalm 51:10 NIV

*W*ise teachers understand the message and share it with their students: A clear conscience is a wonderful thing to possess. It is the reward we earn when we obey God's Word and follow His will. When we follow God's commandments, our earthly rewards are never-ceasing, and our heavenly rewards are everlasting.

To go against one's conscience is neither safe nor right. Here I stand. I cannot do otherwise.

—*Martin Luther*

—A PRAYER—

*D*ear Lord...You speak to me through the Bible, through teachers, and through friends. And, Father, You speak to me through that still, small voice that warns me when I stray from Your will. In these quiet moments and throughout the day, show me Your plan for my life, Lord, that I might serve You.

—*Amen*

CONTENTMENT

But godliness with contentment is great gain. For we brought nothing into the world, and we can take nothing out of it. But if we have food and clothing, we will be content with that.

—1 Timothy 6:6-8 NIV

Keep your lives free from the love of money and be content with what you have, because God has said, "Never will I leave you; never will I forsake you."

—Hebrews 13:5 NIV

I have learned, in whatsoever state I am, therewith to be content.

—Philippians 4:11 KJV

I know what it is to be in need, and I know what it is to have plenty. I have learned the secret of being content in any and every situation, whether well fed or hungry, whether living in plenty or in want. I can do everything through him who gives me strength.

—Philippians 4:12-13 NIV

*G*enuine contentment is never the result of wealth, or power, or fame. The "peace that passes all understanding" is a gift from God to those who trust in Him and follow His commandments. When God becomes the cornerstone of our lives, and when we learn to trust Him completely, contentment will belong to us just as surely as we belong to God.

When you accept rather than fight your circumstances, even though you don't understand them, you open your heart's gate to God's love, peace, joy, and contentment.

—*Amy Carmichael*

—A PRAYER—

*F*ather, show me how to be ambitious in Your work. Let me strive to do Your will here on earth, and as I do, let me find contentment and balance. Let me live in the light of Your will and Your priorities for my life, and when I have done my best, Lord, give me the wisdom to place my faith and my trust in You.

—*Amen*

COURAGE

The LORD himself goes before you and will be with you; he will never leave you nor forsake you. Do not be afraid; do not be discouraged.

—Deuteronomy 31:8 NIV

So do not fear, for I am with you; do not be dismayed, for I am your God. I will strengthen you and help you; I will uphold you with my righteous right hand.

—Isaiah 41:10 NIV

Peace I leave with you, my peace I give unto you: not as the world giveth, give I unto you. Let not your heart be troubled, neither let it be afraid.

—John 14:27 KJV

In thee, O Lord, do I put my trust; let me never be put into confusion.

—Psalm 71:1 KJV

I can do everything through him that gives me strength.

—Philippians 4:13 NIV

*E*very life, like every teaching career, is a tapestry of events: some grand, some not-so-grand, and some downright disappointing. When we reach the mountaintops of life, praising God is easy. But, when the storm clouds form overhead and we find ourselves in the dark valley of despair, our faith is stretched, sometimes to the breaking point. As Christians, we can be comforted: Wherever we find ourselves, whether at the top of the mountain or in the depths of the valley, God is there, and because He cares for us, we can live courageously.

If a person fears God, he or she has no reason to fear anything else. On the other hand, if a person does not fear God, then fear becomes a way of life.
—Beth Moore

—A Prayer—

*G*od, sometimes I face disappointments and challenges that leave me worried and afraid. When I am fearful, let me seek Your strength. When I am anxious, give me faith. Keep me mindful, Lord, that You are my God. With You by my side, Lord, I have nothing to fear. Help me to be Your grateful and courageous teacher this day and every day.

—Amen

DISCIPLINE

He who heeds discipline shows the way to life, but whoever ignores correction leads others astray.

—Proverbs 10:17 NIV

Folly is loud; she is undisciplined and without knowledge.

—Proverbs 9:13 NIV

Whoever gives heed to instruction prospers, and blessed is he that trusts in the Lord.

—Proverbs 16:20 NIV

My son, do not make light of the Lord's discipline, and do not lose heart when he rebukes you, because the Lord disciplines those he loves, and he punishes everyone he accepts as a son.

—Hebrews 12:5 NIV

No discipline seems pleasant at the time, but painful. Later on, however, it produces a harvest of righteousness and peace for those who have been trained by it.

—Hebrews 12:11 NIV

*E*ven the most mild-mannered teachers must, on occasion, dispense discipline to unruly students. The Bible reminds us again and again of God's intention that His children (of all ages) lead disciplined lives. God doesn't reward laziness or misbehavior. To the contrary, He expects His own to adopt a disciplined approach to their lives, and He punishes those who disobey His commandments. Wise teachers preach the gospel of a disciplined lifestyle by word and by example, but not necessarily in that order.

God "longs to be gracious" to us (Isaiah 30:18), and He carries out His judgment against our sin with holy sorrow, intending His discipline to be a vehicle of mercy toward us.

—Nancy Groom

—A Prayer—

*L*ord, Your Holy Word tells us that You expect Your children to be diligent and disciplined. You have told us that the fields are ripe and the workers are few. Lead me to Your fields, Lord, and make me a disciplined worker in Your service. When I am weary, give me strength. When I am discouraged, give me hope. Make me a disciplined, courageous, industrious servant for Your Kingdom today and forever.

—Amen

ENCOURAGING OTHERS

Let the word of Christ dwell in you richly in all wisdom; teaching and admonishing one another in psalms and hymns and spiritual songs, singing with grace in your hearts to the Lord.

—Colossians 3:16 KJV

Let us consider how to stimulate one another to love and good deeds.

—Hebrews 10:24 NASB

Reckless words pierce like a sword, but the tongue of the wise brings healing.

—Proverbs 12:18 NIV

Do not let any unwholesome talk come out of your mouths, but only what is helpful for building others up according to their needs, that it may benefit those who listen.

—Ephesians 4:29 NIV

We urge you, brethren, admonish the unruly, encourage the fainthearted, help the weak, be patient with everyone.

—1 Thessalonians 5:14 NASB

*L*ife is a team sport, and all of us need occasional pats on the back from our teammates and our coaches. Great teachers, like great coaches, inspire their students to learn, to work, to grow, and to persevere. And, never has the need been greater for teachers who understand the art of encouragement. Today's world can be a difficult and uncertain place. Many of our students are in desperate need of a smile or an encouraging word, and since we don't always know who needs our help, the best strategy is to encourage all those who cross our paths. As followers of the Man from Galilee, we can do no less.

He climbs highest who helps another up.

—*Zig Ziglar*

—A Prayer—

*D*ear Heavenly Father, because I am Your child, I am blessed. You have loved me eternally, cared for me faithfully, and saved me through the gift of Your Son Jesus. Just as You have lifted me up, Lord, let me lift up others in a spirit of encouragement and optimism and hope. And, if I can help my students, even in a small way, Dear Lord, may the glory be Yours.

—*Amen*

ENERGY

Never be lacking in zeal, but keep your spiritual fervor, serving the Lord.

—Romans 12:11 NIV

Those who hope in the LORD will renew their strength. They will soar on wings like eagles; they will run and not grow weary, they will walk and not be faint.

—Isaiah 40:31 NIV

The plans of the diligent lead to profit.

—Proverbs 21:5 NIV

He did it with all his heart, and prospered.

—2 Chronicles 31:21 KJV

And whatsoever ye do, do it heartily.

—Colossians 3:23 KJV

If you're a teacher with too many demands and too few hours in which to meet them, you are not alone. Teaching can be a demanding profession. But don't fret. Instead, focus upon God and upon His love for you. Then, ask Him for the strength you need to fulfill your responsibilities. God will give you the energy to do the most important things on today's to-do list…if you ask Him. So ask Him.

When the dream of our heart is one that God has planted there, a strange happiness flows into us. At that moment, all of the spiritual resources of the universe are released to help us. Our praying is then at one with the will of God and becomes a channel for the Creator's purposes for us and our world.

—*Catherine Marshall*

—A Prayer—

Lord, let me find my strength in You. When I am weary, give me rest. When I feel overwhelmed, let me look to You for my priorities. Let Your power be my power, Lord, and let Your way be my way, today and forever.

—*Amen*

FAITH

Have faith in the LORD your God and you will be upheld....

—*2 Chronicles 20:20 NIV*

Now faith is being sure of what we hope for and certain of what we do not see.

—*Hebrews 11:1 NIV*

But without faith it is impossible to please him: for he that cometh to God must believe that he is, and that he is a rewarder of them that diligently seek him.

—*Hebrews 11:6 KJV*

Faith without works is dead....

—*James 2:20 KJV*

Anything is possible if you have faith.

—*Mark 9:23 TLB*

When a suffering woman sought healing by merely touching the hem of His cloak, Jesus replied, "Daughter, be of good comfort; thy faith hath made thee whole" (Matthew 9:24 KJV). The message is clear: if we are to be made whole by God, we must live by faith. But, when we face adversity, illness, or heartbreak, living by faith can be difficult indeed. Still, God remains faithful to us, and we should remain faithful to Him. When we do, we not only glorify God, we also serve as worthy examples to those whom we teach.

The whole person plays a part in true saving faith. The mind understands the truth; the heart desires the truth; and the will acts upon the truth. Faith is not believing in spite of evidence; faith is obeying in spite of consequence.

—*Warren Wiersbe*

—A PRAYER—

Dear God, sometimes this world can be a fearful place, full of uncertainty and doubt. In those dark moments, help me to remember that You are always near and that You can overcome any challenge. Give me faith and let me remember always that with Your love and Your power, I can live courageously and faithfully today and every day.

—*Amen*

FORGIVENESS

For if you forgive men when they sin against you, your heavenly Father will also forgive you. But if you do not forgive men their sins, your Father will not forgive your sins.

—*Matthew 6:14-15 NIV*

Praise the Lord, I tell myself, and never forget the good things he does for me. He forgives all my sins and heals all my diseases.

—*Psalm 103:3 NLT*

Therefore, if you are offering your gift at the altar and there remember that your brother has something against you, leave your gift there in front of the altar. First go and be reconciled to your brother, then come and offer your gift.

—*Matthew 5:23-24 NIV*

And be ye kind one to another, tenderhearted, forgiving one another, even as God for Christ's sake hath forgiven you.

—*Ephesians 4:32 KJV*

*F*orgiveness is God's commandment, but oh how difficult a commandment it can be to follow. Being frail, fallible, imperfect human beings, we are quick to anger, quick to blame, slow to forgive, and even slower to forget. No matter. Forgiveness, although difficult, is God's way. Teachers, having been placed in positions of leadership, serve as important role models to their students. As such, teachers must be models of forgiveness, both inside the classroom and out.

Our Savior kneels down and gazes upon the darkest acts of our lives. But rather than recoil in horror, he reaches out in kindness and says, "I can clean that if you want." And, from the basin of his grace, he scoops a palm full of mercy and washes our sin.

—*Max Lucado*

—A Prayer—

*F*ather, sometimes I am tempted to strike out at those who have hurt me. Keep me mindful that forgiveness is Your commandment. You have forgiven me, Lord; let me show my thankfulness to You by offering forgiveness to others. And, when I do, may others see Your love reflected through my words and deeds.

—*Amen*

GENEROSITY

...so let him give; not grudgingly, or of necessity: for God loveth a cheerful giver.

—2 Corinthians 9:7 KJV

Above all, love each other deeply, because love covers a multitude of sins.

—1 Peter 4:8 NIV

The man with two tunics should share with him who has none, and the one who has food should do the same.

—Luke 3:11 NIV

I tell you the truth, whatever you did for one of the least of these brothers of mine, you did for me.

—Matthew 25:40 NIV

The good person is generous and lends lavishly....

—Psalm 112:5 MSG

The thread of generosity is thoroughly woven into the very fabric of Christ's teachings. And, because we live in a world that has enormous needs, we believers have a profound responsibility to share our possessions, both spiritual and material. How can we, as teachers, encourage our students to give freely of *their* possessions? The answer is simple: by giving freely of our own.

It's not difficult to make an impact on your world. All you really have to do is put the needs of others ahead of your own. You can make a difference with a little time and a big heart.

—*James Dobson*

—A PRAYER—

Father…Your gifts are beyond comprehension. You gave Your Son Jesus to save us, and Your motivation was love. I pray that the gifts I give my students will come from an overflow of my heart, and that they will echo the great love You have for all of Your children.

—*Amen*

GIFTS

Every good gift and every perfect gift is from above, and cometh down from the Father of lights.

—James 1:17 KJV

Now there are varieties of gifts, but the same Spirit. And there are varieties of ministries, and the same Lord.

—1 Corinthians 12:4-5 NASB

Do not neglect the spiritual gift that is within you....

—1 Timothy 4:14 NASB

Since we have gifts that differ according to the grace given to us, let each exercise them accordingly: if prophecy, according to the proportion of his faith; if service, in his serving; or he who teaches, in his teaching; or he who exhorts, in his exhortation; he who gives, with liberality; he who leads, with diligence; he who shows mercy, with cheerfulness.

—Romans 12:6-8 NASB

*P*erhaps you are one of the teachers who have a natural gift for leading a class. But, even if you have the oratorical skills of Churchill and the mind of Einstein, you can still improve your teaching skills…and you should. God's gifts are no guarantee of success; they must be cultivated and nurtured; otherwise they diminish over time. Today, accept this challenge: value the gift that God has given you, nourish it, make it grow, and share it with your students and with the world. After all, the best way to say "Thank You" for God's gifts is to use them.

God is still in the process of dispensing gifts, and He uses ordinary individuals like us to develop those gifts in other people.

—Howard Hendricks

—A Prayer—

*L*ord, You have given all of us talents, and I am no exception. You have blessed me with a gift—let me discover it, nurture it, and use it to the glory of Your Kingdom. Today, let me be a good and faithful steward, Father, of my talents and my possessions. Let me share my gifts with the world, and let me offer praise to You, the Giver of all things good.

—Amen

GOD'S BLESSINGS

For surely, O LORD, you bless the righteous; you surround them with your favor as with a shield.

—Psalm 5:12 NIV

I will bless them and the places surrounding my hill. I will send down showers in season; there will be showers of blessings.

—Ezekiel 34:26 NIV

I will make you into a great nation and I will bless you; I will make your name great, and you will be a blessing. I will bless those who bless you, and whoever curses you I will curse; and all peoples on earth will be blessed through you.

—Genesis 12:2-3 NIV

The Lord is kind and merciful, slow to get angry, full of unfailing love. The Lord is good to everyone. He showers compassion on all his creation.

—Psalm 145:8-9 NLT

*I*f you sat down and began counting your blessings, how long would it take? A very, very long time! Your blessings include life, freedom, family, friends, talents, possessions, and, of course, the opportunity that you have been given to become a teacher. But, your greatest blessing—a gift that is yours for the asking—is God's gift of salvation through Christ Jesus. Today, give thanks for your blessings and show your thanks by using them and by sharing them. When you do, God will smile...and so will your students.

∝

Jesus intended for us to be overwhelmed by the blessings of regular days. He said it was the reason he had come: "I am come that they might have life, and that they might have it more abundantly."

—Gloria Gaither

—A Prayer—

*L*ord, You have given me so much, and I am thankful. Today, I seek Your blessings for my life, and I know that every good thing You give me is to be shared with my students. I am blessed that I might be a blessing to those around me, Father. Let me give thanks for Your gifts...and let me share them.

—Amen

GOD'S COMMANDMENTS

Jesus answered and said unto him, If a man love me, he will keep my words: and my Father will love him, and we will come unto him, and make our abode with him.

—John 14:23 KJV

Happy are those who fear the Lord. Yes, happy are those who delight in doing what he commands.

—Psalm 112:1 NLT

For this is the love of God, that we keep his commandments....

—1 John 5:3 KJV

Whoso despiseth the word shall be destroyed: but he that feareth the commandment shall be rewarded.

—Proverbs 13:13 KJV

He that hath my commandments, and keepeth them, he it is that loveth me: and he that loveth me shall be loved of my Father, and I will love him, and will manifest myself to him.

—John 14:21 KJV

*R*ighteous living has many components: faith, honesty, generosity, discipline, love, kindness, humility, gratitude, and worship, to name but a few. If we seek to follow the steps of Jesus, we must seek to live according to His commandments. In short, we must, to the best of our abilities, live according to the principles contained in God's Holy Word. And then, through our words and our deeds, we must teach our students to do the same.

Let us remember therefore this lesson: That to worship our God sincerely we must evermore begin by hearkening to His voice, and by giving ear to what He commands us. For if every man goes after his own way, we shall wander. We may well run, but we shall never be a whit nearer to the right way, but rather farther away from it.

—*John Calvin*

—A Prayer—

*T*hank You, Dear Lord, for loving me enough to give me rules to live by. Let me live by Your commandments, and let me lead those I teach to do the same. Let me walk righteously in Your way, Dear Lord, today and always.

—*Amen*

GOD'S GRACE

But by the grace of God I am what I am, and his grace to me was not without effect.

—*1 Corinthians 15:10 NIV*

You therefore, my son, be strong in the grace that is in Christ Jesus.

—*2 Timothy 2:1 NKJV*

And God raised us up with Christ and seated us with him in the heavenly realms in Christ Jesus, in order that in the coming ages he might show the incomparable riches of his grace, expressed in his kindness to us in Christ Jesus.

—*Ephesians 2:6-7 NIV*

For the law was given through Moses; grace and truth came through Jesus Christ.

—*John 1:17 NIV*

My grace is sufficient for you, for my power is made perfect in weakness.

—*2 Corinthians 12:9 NIV*

We have not earned our salvation; it is a gift from God. When we accept Christ as our Savior, we are saved by God's grace. Let us praise God for His gift, and let us share the Good News with all who cross our paths. God's grace is the ultimate gift, and we owe to Him the ultimate in thanksgiving. We demonstrate our thanks by sharing His message and His love.

The grace of God is sufficient for all our needs, for every problem, and for every difficulty, for every broken heart, and for every human sorrow.

—*Peter Marshall*

—A PRAYER—

Lord, accepting Your grace can be hard. Somehow, I feel that I must earn Your love and Your acceptance. Yet, the Bible promises that You love me and save me by Your grace. It is a gift I can only accept and cannot earn. Thank You for Your priceless, everlasting gift.

—*Amen*

GOD'S LOVE

For God so loved the world, that he gave his only begotten Son, that whosoever believeth in him should not perish, but have everlasting life.

—John 3:16 KJV

But the love of the Lord remains forever with those who fear him. His salvation extends to the children's children of those who are faithful to his covenant, of those who obey his commandments!

—Psalm 103:17-18 NLT

Praise him, all you people of the earth, for he loves us with unfailing love; the faithfulness of the Lord endures forever. Praise the Lord!

—Psalm 117 NLT

But God demonstrates his own love for us in this: While we were still sinners, Christ died for us.

—Romans 5:8 NIV

His banner over me was love.

—Song of Solomon 2:4 KJV

*G*od is a loving Father. We are God's children, and we are called upon to be faithful to Him. We return our Father's love by sharing it with others. We honor our Heavenly Father by obeying His commandments and sharing His message. When we do, we are blessed…and the Father smiles.

God loves us the way we are, but He loves us too much to leave us that way.

—Leighton Ford

—A Prayer—

*G*od, You are love. I love You, Lord, and as I love You more, I am able to love my family and friends and students more. Let me be Your loving servant, Heavenly Father, today and throughout eternity.

—Amen

GOD'S MERCY

Praise be to the God and Father of our Lord Jesus Christ! In his great mercy he has given us new birth into a living hope through the resurrection of Jesus Christ from the dead....

—*1 Peter 1:3 NIV*

For the LORD your God is a merciful God....

—*Deuteronomy 4:31 NIV*

But because of his great love for us, God, who is rich in mercy, made us alive with Christ even when we were dead in transgressions—it is by grace you have been saved.

—*Ephesians 2:4-5 NIV*

But the mercy of the LORD is from everlasting to everlasting upon them that fear him, and his righteousness unto children's children....

—*Psalm 103:17 KJV*

O praise the LORD, all ye nations: praise him, all ye people. For his merciful kindness is great toward us: and the truth of the LORD endureth for ever. Praise ye the LORD.

—*Psalm 117 KJV*

$\mathcal{R}$omans 3:23 reminds us of a universal truth that we already know: "All have sinned, and come short of the glory of God...." And, despite our imperfections, God sent His Son to die for our sins. As Christians, we have been blessed by a merciful, loving God, and one way that we thank God is to share His love and His mercy with our students and with all others whom God chooses to place in our paths.

God's heart of mercy provides for us not only pardon from sin but also a daily provision of spiritual food to strengthen us.

—Jim Cymbala

—A Prayer—

$\mathcal{D}$ear Lord, You have blessed me with so much: Your love, Your mercy, and Your grace. Enable me to be merciful toward others, Father, just as You have been merciful toward me so that I might share Your love with all those I teach.

—Amen

GOD'S PLAN

Who are those who fear the Lord? He will show them the path they should choose. They will live in prosperity, and their children will inherit the Promised Land.

—*Psalm 25:12-13 NLT*

The steps of the godly are directed by the Lord. He delights in every detail of their lives. Though they stumble, they will not fall, for the Lord holds them by the hand.

—*Psalm 37:23-24 NLT*

It is God who works in you to will and to act according to his good purpose.

—*Philippians 2:13 NIV*

"For I know the plans I have for you," declares the Lord, "plans to prosper you and not to harm you, plans to give you hope and a future. Then you will call upon me and come and pray to me, and I will listen to you."

—*Jeremiah 29:11-12 NIV*

*G*od has plans for your life *and* for the lives of your students. Big plans. But He won't force His plans upon you. To the contrary, He has given all of His children free will (a fact that is not lost on any teacher who has ever tried to quiet an unruly classroom). While you, as a concerned teacher, can encourage your students to seek purpose and meaning for their own lives, you can't force them to do so. You can, however, seek to discover God's plan for *your* life. God is listening and waiting for You to reach out to Him, and He intends to use you in wonderful, unexpected ways.

God has a course mapped out for your life, and all the inadequacies in the world will not change His mind. He will be with you every step of the way. And though it may take time, He has a celebration planned for when you cross over the "Red Seas" of your life.

—Chuck Swindoll

—A Prayer—

*D*ear Lord, let me choose Your plans. You created me, and You have called me to do Your work here on earth. Today, I choose to seek Your will and to live it, knowing that when I trust in You, I am eternally blessed.

—Amen

GOD'S SUPPORT

The LORD is my strength and song, and He has become my salvation; He is my God, and I will praise Him....

—Exodus 15:2 NKJV

But my God shall supply all your need according to his riches in glory by Christ Jesus.

—Philippians 4:19 KJV

The Lord is my rock, my fortress and my savior; my God is my rock in whom I find protection. He is my shield, the strength of my salvation, and my stronghold.

—Psalm 18:2 NLT

So, what do you think? With God on our side like this, how can we lose? If God didn't hesitate to put everything on the line for us, embracing our condition and exposing himself to the worst by sending his own Son, is there anything else he wouldn't gladly and freely do for us?

—Romans 8:31-32 MSG

God loves us and protects us. In times of trouble, he comforts us; in times of sorrow, He dries our tears. When we are troubled, or weak, or sorrowful, God is as near as our next breath. Let us build our lives on the rock that cannot be shaken...let us trust in God. And, let us share the Good News of His Son with a world that needs His grace and His love.

If we are beset by an unseen foe, we are also befriended by an Unseen Friend. Great is our adversary, but greater is our ally.

—*Vance Havner*

—A PRAYER—

Heavenly Father, You never leave or forsake me. You are always with me, protecting me and encouraging me. Whatever this day may bring, I thank You for Your love and Your strength. Let me lean upon You, Father, this day and forever.

—*Amen*

GOD'S TIMING

He [Jesus] said to them: "It is not for you to know the times or dates the Father has set by his own authority."

—*Acts 1:7 NIV*

He has made everything beautiful in its time. He has also set eternity in the hearts of men; yet they cannot fathom what God has done from beginning to end.

—*Ecclesiastes 3:11 NIV*

Yet the LORD longs to be gracious to you; he rises to show you compassion. For the LORD is a God of justice. Blessed are all who wait for him!

—*Isaiah 30:18 NIV*

I wait for the LORD, my soul waits, and in his word I put my hope.

—*Psalm 130:5 NIV*

I waited patiently for the LORD; And He inclined to me, And heard my cry.

—*Psalm 40:1 NKJV*

Students, as a whole, can be quite an impatient lot. They can't wait for class to end; ditto for the school day and the school week. They wait impatiently for Christmas vacation, spring break, and—most urgently—summer vacation. But, wise teachers understand that life beyond the classroom requires patience, patience, and more patience. Unlike the precisely charted school year, life unfolds according to a timetable that is ordained, not by man, but by God. Let us, as believers, wait patiently for God, and let us teach patience to those who look to us for guidance...even if they're squirming in their seats, waiting for the bell to ring.

God never hurries. There are no deadlines against which He must work. To know this is to quiet our spirits and relax our nerves.

—*A. W. Tozer*

—A Prayer—

Lord...Your timing is seldom the same as my timing, but Your timing is always right for me. You are my Father, and You have a plan for my life that is grander than I can imagine. When I am impatient, remind me that You are never early or late. You are always on time, Lord, so let me trust in You...always.

—*Amen*

GOLDEN RULE

Let us not become weary in doing good, for at the proper time we will reap a harvest if we do not give up.

—*Galatians 6:9 NIV*

Each of you should look not only to your own interests, but also to the interest of others.

—*Philippians 2:4 NIV*

So in everything, do to others what you would have them do to you, for this sums up the Law and the Prophets.

—*Matthew 7:12 NIV*

Give to everyone who asks you, and if anyone takes what belongs to you, do not demand it back.

—*Luke 6:30 NIV*

Carry each other's burdens, and in this way you will fulfill the law of Christ.

—*Galatians 6:2 NIV*

The Golden Rule is God's rule. Today spread a heaping helping of kindness wherever you go. Make forgiveness a cornerstone of your dealings with others; treat others with the same courtesy that you expect from them; be generous with your time and your possessions. When you do, you'll discover that the more kindness you give away to others, the more you'll receive in return. And, you'll become a shining example to your students who, by the way, are watching you…and learning from you.

The best portion of a good man's life is his little, nameless, unremembered acts of kindness and of love.

—*William Wordsworth*

—A PRAYER—

Dear Lord, let me treat others as I wish to be treated. Because I expect kindness, let me be kind. Because I wish to be loved, let me be loving. Because I need forgiveness, let me be merciful. In all things, Lord, let me live by the Golden Rule, and let me teach that rule to others through my words and my deeds.

—*Amen*

GRATITUDE

As you therefore have received Christ Jesus the Lord, so walk in Him, having been firmly rooted and now being built up in Him and established in your faith, just as you were instructed, and overflowing with gratitude.

—*Colossians 2:6-7 NASB*

Enter his gates with thanksgiving, go into his courts with praise. Give thanks to him and bless his name.

—*Psalm 100:4 NLT*

Everything created by God is good, and nothing is to be rejected, if it is received with gratitude; for it is sanctified by means of the word of God and prayer.

—*1 Timothy 4:4-5 NASB*

Therefore, since we receive a kingdom which cannot be shaken, let us show gratitude, by which we may offer to God an acceptable service with reverence and awe....

—*Hebrews 12:28 NASB*

For most of us, life is complicated and busy. And, as teachers, we have countless responsibilities that begin long before the school bell rings and end long after the last student has left the classroom. Amid the rush and crush of the daily grind, it is easy to lose sight of God and His blessings. But, when we forget to slow down and say "Thank You" to our Maker, we rob ourselves of His presence, His peace, and His joy. Instead of ignoring God, we should praise Him many times each day. Then, with gratitude in our hearts, we can face the day's complications with the perspective and power that only He can provide.

It is only with gratitude that life becomes rich.
—*Dietrich Bonhoeffer*

—A Prayer—

Dear Jesus, I know that You are the bread of life and the Savior of my life. When I am weak, You give me strength, and when I am worried, You give me peace. Thank You, Lord, for the gift of eternal life and for the gift of eternal love. May I be ever grateful, and may I share Your good news with a world that so desperately needs Your healing grace.

—*Amen*

HONESTY

...as we have received mercy, we faint not; but have renounced the hidden things of dishonesty, not walking in craftiness, nor handling the word of God deceitfully; but, by manifestation of the truth, commending ourselves to every man's conscience in the sight of God.

—2 Corinthians 4:1-2 KJV

Therefore laying aside falsehood, speak truth, each one of you, with his neighbor, for we are members of one another.

—Ephesians 4:25 NASB

But when he, the Spirit of truth, comes, he will guide you into all truth....

—John 16:13 NIV

Jesus answered, "I am the way and the truth and the life. No one comes to the Father except through me."

—John 14:6 NIV

And ye shall know the truth, and the truth shall make you free.

—John 8:32 KJV

From the time we are children, we are taught that honesty is the best policy. And, in the classroom, we instruct our students that honesty is also the school's policy. But, honesty is not just *the best* policy or *the school's* policy, it is also *God's* policy. If we are to be servants worthy of His holy blessings, we must remember that truth is not just the best way, it is God's way. May we teach truth and practice it…but not necessarily in that order.

❧

Honesty has a beautiful and refreshing simplicity about it. No ulterior motives. No hidden meanings. As honesty and integrity characterize our lives, there will be no need to manipulate others.

—*Chuck Swindoll*

—A Prayer—

Dear Lord, You command Your children to walk in truth. Let me follow Your commandment. Give me the courage to speak honestly, and let me walk righteously with You so that students might see Your eternal truth reflected in my words and my deeds.

—*Amen*

HOPE

Be of good courage, and he shall strengthen your heart, all ye that hope in the LORD.

—Psalm 31:24 KJV

Be joyful in hope, patient in affliction, faithful in prayer.

—Romans 12:12 NIV

The Lord is good to those whose hope is in him, to the one who seeks him; it is good to wait quietly for the salvation of the Lord.

—Lamentations 3:25-26 NIV

Blessed is he whose help is the God of Jacob, whose hope is in the LORD his God, the Maker of heaven and earth, the sea, and everything in them—the LORD, who remains faithful forever.

—Psalm 146:5-6 NIV

May the God of hope fill you with all joy and peace as you trust in him, so that you may overflow with hope by the power of the Holy Spirit.

—Romans 15:13 NIV

Despite God's promises, despite Christ's love, and despite our countless blessings, we frail human beings can still lose hope from time to time. When we do, we need the encouragement of Christian friends, the life-changing power of prayer, and the healing truth of God's Holy Word. If we find ourselves falling into the spiritual traps of worry and discouragement, we should seek the healing touch of Jesus and the encouraging words of fellow Christians. Even though this world can be a place of trials and struggles, God has promised us peace, joy, and eternal life *if* we give ourselves to Him. And, of course, God keeps His promises today, tomorrow, and forever.

In the washroom, we need a soap dispenser. In the classroom, we need a hope dispenser.

—Marie T. Freeman

—A Prayer—

Today, Dear Lord, I will live in hope. If I become discouraged, I will turn to You. If I grow weary, I will seek strength in You. In every aspect of my life, I will trust You. You are my Father, Lord, and I place my hope and my faith in You.

—Amen

+++
JOY
+++

Rejoice, and be exceeding glad: for great is your reward in heaven....

—Matthew 5:12 KJV

Thou wilt show me the path of life: in thy presence is fulness of joy; at thy right hand there are pleasures for evermore.

—Psalm 16:11 KJV

Weeping may endure for a night, but joy cometh in the morning.

—Psalm 30:5 KJV

I will thank you, Lord, with all my heart; I will tell of all the marvelous things you have done. I will be filled with joy because of you. I will sing praises to your name, O Most High.

—Psalm 9:1-2 NLT

Delight thyself also in the LORD; and he shall give thee the desires of thine heart.

—Psalm 37:4 KJV

*C*hrist made it clear to His followers: He intended that His joy would become their joy. And it still holds true today: Christ intends that His believers share His love with His joy in their hearts. Today, whether you find yourself inside the classroom or outside it, share the joy that you feel in *your* heart, just as Christ freely shared His joy with you.

To choose joy means the determination to let whatever takes place bring us one step closer to the God of life.

—Henri Nouwen

—A PRAYER—

*D*ear Lord, You have created a glorious universe that is far beyond my understanding. You have given me the gift of Your Son and the gift of salvation. Let me be a joyful Christian, Lord, this day and every day. Today is Your gift to me. Let me use it to Your glory as I give all the praise to You.

—Amen

THE JOY OF TEACHING

Hear, O Israel: The LORD our God, the LORD is one. Love the LORD your God with all your heart and with all your soul and with all your strength. These commandments that I give you today are to be upon your hearts. Impress them on your children. Talk about them when you sit at home and when you walk along the road, when you lie down and when you get up.

—Deuteronomy 6:4-7 NIV

These things have I spoken unto you, that my joy might remain in you, and that your joy might be full.

—John 15:11 KJV

These things I speak in the world, that they might have my joy fulfilled in themselves.

—John 17:13 KJV

Light shines on the godly, and joy on those who do right. May all who are godly be happy in the Lord and praise his holy name.

—Psalm 97:11-12 NLT

*J*esus Christ promises that we can have abundance through Him. Of course, teaching should be a joyful experience, but every teacher knows that some days are so busy and so hurried that abundance seems a distant promise. It is not. Every day, we can claim the spiritual abundance and joy that God promises for our lives...and we should.

❧

There's no word in the language I revere more than "teacher." My heart sings when a kid refers to me as his teacher, and it always has. I've honored myself and the entire family of man by becoming a teacher.

—*Pat Conroy*

—A Prayer—

*D*ear Lord...You are my strength and my joy. I will rejoice in the day that You have made, and I will give thanks for the countless blessings that You have given me. Let me be a joyful teacher, Father, and let me praise You for all the marvelous things You have done.

—*Amen*

KINDNESS

Refuse to get involved in inane discussions; they always end up in fights. God's servant must not be argumentative, but a gentle listener and a teacher who keeps cool, working firmly but patiently with those who refuse to obey.

—2 Timothy 2:23-24 MSG

A gentle answer turns away wrath, but a harsh word stirs up anger.

—Proverbs 15:1 NIV

I tell you the truth, whatever you did for one of the least of these brothers of mine, you did for me.

—Matthew 25:40 NIV

And be ye kind one to another, tenderhearted, forgiving one another, even as God for Christ's sake hath forgiven you.

—Ephesians 4:32 KJV

*G*odly teachers share the same lesson all over the world: kindness. Christ taught the very same message when He spoke the words recorded in Matthew 7:12. The Golden Rule commands us to treat others as we wish to be treated. When we weave the thread of kindness into the very fabric of our lives, we give glory to the One who gave His life for us.

Kind words can be short and easy to speak, but their echoes are truly endless.

—Mother Teresa

—A Prayer—

*L*ord, sometimes this world can become a place of busyness, frustration, and confusion. Slow me down, Lord, that I might see the needs of those around me, especially my students. Today, help me show mercy to those in need. Today, let me spread kind words of thanksgiving and celebration in honor of Your Son. Today, let forgiveness rule my heart. And every day, Lord, let my love for Christ be reflected through deeds of kindness for those who need the healing touch of the Master's hand.

—Amen

KNOWLEDGE

By wisdom a house is built, and through understanding it is established; through knowledge its rooms are filled with rare and beautiful treasures.

—Proverbs 24:3-4 NIV

It is not good to have zeal without knowledge, nor to be hasty and miss the way.

—Proverbs 19:2 NIV

The fear of the Lord is the beginning of knowledge, but fools despise wisdom and discipline.

—Proverbs 1:7 NIV

The lips of the wise spread knowledge; not so the hearts of fools.

—Proverbs 15:7 NIV

The knowledge of the secrets of the kingdom of heaven has been given to you....

—Matthew 13:11 NIV

*O*ur children need both knowledge and wisdom. Knowledge is found in textbooks. Wisdom, on the other hand, is found in God's Holy Word and in the carefully chosen words of loving parents and thoughtful teachers. When we give our children the gift of knowledge, we do them a wonderful service. But, when we share the gift of wisdom, we offer a timeless treasure that surpasses knowledge and reshapes eternity.

A teacher affects eternity; he can never tell where his influence stops.

—Henry Adams

—A Prayer—

*L*ord, You are my Teacher. Help me to be a student of Your Word and a servant of Your will. Let me live by the truth You reveal, let me trust in the wisdom of Your commandments, and let me teach others the glory of Your ways.

—Amen

LAUGHTER

There is a time for everything, and a season for every activity under heaven...a time to weep and a time to laugh, a time to mourn and a time to dance....

—*Ecclesiastes 3:1,4 NIV*

Shout for joy to the LORD, all the earth, burst into jubilant song with music; make music to the LORD with the harp, with the harp and the sound of singing, with trumpets and the blast of the ram's horn—shout for joy before the LORD, the King.

—*Psalm 98:4-6 NIV*

Nehemiah said, "Go and enjoy choice food and sweet drinks, and send some to those who have nothing prepared. This day is sacred to our Lord. Do not grieve, for the joy of the LORD is your strength."

—*Nehemiah 8:10 NIV*

Clap your hands, all you nations; shout to God with cries of joy.

—*Psalm 47:1 NIV*

It has been said, quite correctly, that laughter is God's medicine. Today, whether you find yourself at school, at home, or at church, approach life with a smile and a chuckle. After all, God created laughter for a reason...and Father indeed knows best. So laugh!

We are all here for a spell, get all the good laughs you can.

—*Will Rogers*

—A PRAYER—

Lord, when I begin to take myself or my life too seriously, let me laugh. When I rush from place to place, slow me down, Lord, and let me laugh. Put a smile on my face, Dear Lord, and let me share that smile with those I teach...and let me laugh.

—*Amen*

LEADERSHIP

His lord said unto him, Well done, thou good and faithful servant: thou hast been faithful over a few things, I will make thee ruler over many things: enter thou into the joy of thy lord.

—*Matthew 25:21 KJV*

We have different gifts, according to the grace given us. If a man's gift is prophesying, let him use it in proportion to his faith. If it is serving, let him serve; if it is teaching, let him teach; if it is encouraging, let him encourage; if it is contributing to the needs of others, let him give generously; if it is leadership, let him govern diligently; if it is showing mercy, let him do it cheerfully.

—*Romans 12:6-8 NIV*

Those who are wise will shine like the brightness of the heavens, and those who lead many to righteousness, like the stars for ever and ever.

—*Daniel 12:3 NIV*

$\mathcal{U}$nless the teacher is the leader of the classroom, effective learning will not take place. If students are to learn, the teacher must assume control. John Maxwell writes, "Great leaders understand that the right attitude will set the right atmosphere, which enables the right response from others." Savvy teachers strike a balance between discipline (which is necessary for maintaining order) and fun (which is necessary for maintaining interest). The rest, of course, is up to the students.

❧

Your enthusiasm will be infectious, stimulating, and attractive to others. They will love you for it. They will go for you and with you.

—Norman Vincent Peale

—A Prayer—

$\mathcal{H}$eavenly Father, Your Word tells us that teachers are judged strictly and that I have an awesome responsibility to lead my students in the way of truth. Lord, I ask for Your help today as I prepare to teach. May I speak the truth, may I be a worthy example to those who watch my behavior, and may the glory be Yours.

—Amen

LIFE

Watch your life and doctrine closely. Persevere in them, because if you do, you will save both yourself and your hearers.

—1 Timothy 4:16 NIV

His divine power has given us everything we need for life and godliness through our knowledge of him who called us by his own glory and goodness.

—2 Peter 1:3 NIV

Seek the Lord, and ye shall live....

—Amos 5:6 KJV

I urge you to live a life worthy of the calling you have received.

—Ephesians 4:1 NIV

And Jesus said unto them, I am the bread of life: he that cometh to me shall never hunger; and he that believeth on me shall never thirst.

—John 6:35 KJV

Each day of our lives, we are confronted with countless opportunities to serve God and to worship Him. When we do, He blesses us. But, when we turn our backs to the Creator, or, when we are simply too busy to acknowledge His greatness, we do ourselves and our students a profound disservice. Life is a glorious opportunity to place ourselves in the service of the One who is the Giver of all blessings. May we seek His will, trust His word, and place Him where He belongs: at the center of our lives.

People, places, and things were never meant to give us life. God alone is the author of a fulfilling life.

—*Gary Smalley & John Trent*

—A PRAYER—

You are the Giver of all life, O Lord, and You created me to have fellowship with You. Let me live a life that pleases You, Lord, and let me thank You always for Your blessings. You love me and protect me, Heavenly Father. Let me be grateful, and let me live for You today and throughout eternity.

—*Amen*

LOVING GOD

We love him, because he first loved us.

—*1 John 4:19 KJV*

This is love: not that we loved God, but that he loved us and sent his Son as an atoning sacrifice for our sins.

—*1 John 4:10 NIV*

Love the LORD your God with all your heart and with all your soul and with all your strength.

—*Deuteronomy 6:5 NIV*

I will sing of the LORD'S great love forever; with my mouth I will make your faithfulness known through all generations.

—*Psalm 89:1 NIV*

And we know that in all things God works for the good of those who love him, who have been called according to his purpose.

—*Romans 8:28 NIV*

C. S. Lewis observed, "A man's spiritual health is exactly proportional to his love for God." If we are to enjoy the spiritual health that God intends for our lives, we must praise Him and love Him. And, this is as it should be...after all, He first loved us.

❧

If you want to know the will and voice of God, you must give the time and effort to cultivate a love relationship with Him. That is what He wants!

—*Henry Blackaby*

—A PRAYER—

Dear Heavenly Father, You have blessed me and my students with a love that is infinite and eternal. May we love You, Lord, more and more each day. Make me a worthy teacher and a loving servant, Dear Lord. And, let me show my love for You by sharing Your message and Your love with all those I teach and with the world.

—*Amen*

LOVING OTHERS

And he has given us this command: Whoever loves God must also love his brother.

—1 John 4:21 NIV

Jesus replied, "'Love the Lord your God with all your heart and with all your soul and with all your mind.' This is the first and greatest commandment. And the second is like it: 'Love your neighbor as yourself.' All the Law and the Prophets hang on these two commandments."

—Matthew 22:37-40 NIV

And the Lord make you to increase and abound in love one toward another, and toward all men....

—1 Thessalonians 3:12 KJV

Above all, love each other deeply, because love covers over a multitude of sins.

—1 Peter 4:8 NIV

Love one another deeply, from the heart.

—1 Peter 1:22 NIV

If we are to follow the commands of our Father in heaven, we must sow seeds of kindness and love. God is love, and kindness is God's commandment. As believers, we are obliged to love *all* our neighbors, not just the loveable ones. So, today, let's be a little kinder than necessary, and let's teach the art of kindness through our words and our deeds. Our students are watching…and so is God.

∽

To love another person is to help them love God.
—*Søren Kierkegaard*

—A Prayer—

Father…You have given me love that is beyond human understanding, and I am Your loving servant. May the love that I feel for You be reflected in the compassion that I show toward my students. Give me Your eyes to see others as You see them, Lord, and let me show compassion and understanding to those I teach this day and every day.

—Amen

Maturity

But grow in grace, and in the knowledge of our Lord and Saviour Jesus Christ....

—2 Peter 3:18 KJV

Continue in what you have learned and have become convinced of, because you know those from whom you learned it, and how from infancy you have known the holy Scriptures, which are able to make you wise for salvation through faith in Christ Jesus.

—2 Timothy 3:14,15 NIV

Consider it pure joy, my brothers, whenever you face trials of many kinds, because you know that the testing of your faith develops perseverance. Perseverance must finish its work so that you may be mature and complete, not lacking anything.

—James 1:2-4 NIV

I press on toward the goal to win the prize for which God has called me heavenward in Christ Jesus.

—Philippians 3:14 NIV

If only students would behave maturely and responsibly, teaching would be a breeze. But, here in the real world, young people don't grow into mature adults overnight. What's a teacher to do? Be patient, be understanding, and be demanding. Teachers who allow undisciplined behavior to go unchecked are doing a disservice to their students. God does not reward laziness nor does He praise mediocrity, and neither should we.

Salvation is the process that's done, that's secure, that no one can take away from you. Sanctification is the lifelong process of being changed from one degree of glory to the next, growing in Christ, putting away the old, taking on the new.

—*Max Lucado*

—A Prayer—

Thank You, Lord, that I am not yet what I am to become. The Holy Scripture says that You are at work in my life, continuing to help me grow and to mature in the faith. Show me Your wisdom, Father, and let me live according to Your Word and Your will.

—*Amen*

MIRACLES

God also testified to it [salvation] by signs, wonders and various miracles, and gifts of the Holy Spirit distributed according to his will.

—Hebrews 2:4 NIV

Jesus said to them, "I have shown you many great miracles from the Father."

—John 10:32 NIV

For with God nothing shall be impossible.

—Luke 1:37 KJV

You are the God who performs miracles; you display your power among the peoples.

—Psalm 77:14 NIV

We are imperfect human beings with limited understanding and limited faith, and, thus, we sometimes place limitations on God. But God's power has no limitations. God is a worker of miracles both great and small, and when we trust Him with everything we have and everything we are, we experience the miraculous results of His endless love and His awesome power.

Faith means believing in realities that go beyond sense and sight. It is the awareness of unseen divine realities all around you.

—Joni Eareckson Tada

—A Prayer—

Heavenly Father, You are the miracle worker of life; let me trust in Your power and Your love. With You, Father, all things are possible. Keep me mindful that You are a God of power and possibilities, and let me never place limitations upon You, the Designer and Creator of the Universe.

—Amen

MISSIONS

Now then we are ambassadors for Christ....

—*2 Corinthians 5:20 KJV*

After these things the Lord appointed other seventy also, and sent them two and two before his face into every city and place, whither he himself would come. Therefore said he unto them, The harvest truly is great, but the laborers are few: pray ye therefore the Lord of the harvest, that he would send forth laborers into his harvest. Go your ways: behold, I send you forth as lambs among wolves.

—*Luke 10:1-3 KJV*

Then Jesus came to them and said, "All authority in heaven and on earth has been given to me. Therefore go and make disciples of all nations, baptizing them in the name of the Father and of the Son and of the Holy Spirit, and teaching them to obey everything I have commanded you. And surely I am with you always, to the very end of the age."

—*Matthew 28:18-20 NIV*

As believers in Christ, we are called to share His Good News with our families, our neighbors, and the world. Jesus commanded His disciples to become fishers of men. We must do likewise. And, the time to go fishing is now.

The Christian life is a matter of coming and going: "Come unto me...." (Matt. 11:28); "Go ye unto the world...." (Mark 16:15).

—*Vance Havner*

—A PRAYER—

Dear Heavenly Father, every man and woman, every boy and girl is Your child. You desire that all Your children know Jesus as their Lord and Savior. Father, let me be part of Your Great Commission. Let me give, let me pray, and let me go out into this world so that I might be a fisher of men...for You.

—*Amen*

MISTAKES

I waited patiently for the LORD; he turned to me and heard my cry. He lifted me out of the slimy pit, out of the mud and mire; he set my feet on a rock and gave me a firm place to stand. He put a new song in my mouth, a hymn of praise to our God....

—Psalm 40:1-3 NIV

You were taught, with regard to your former way of life, to put off your old self, which is being corrupted by its deceitful desires; to be made new in the attitude of your minds; and to put on the new self, created to be like God in true righteousness and holiness.

—Ephesians 4:22-24 NIV

If we confess our sins, he is faithful and just and will forgive us our sins and purify us from all unrighteousness.

—1 John 1:9 NIV

Have mercy on me, O God, according to your unfailing love; according to your great compassion blot out my transgressions. Wash away all my iniquity and cleanse me from my sin.

—Psalm 51:1-2 NIV

$\mathscr{E}$very teacher who has ever graded a paper understands that the old saying is true: "To err is human…." Yes, we human beings—students and teachers alike—are inclined to make mistakes, and lots of them. When we commit the inevitable blunders of life, let us be quick to correct our errors. And, when we are hurt by the mistakes of others, let us be quick to forgive, just as God has forgiven us.

Lord, when we are wrong, make us willing to change; and when we are right, make us easy to live with.

—*Peter Marshall*

—A PRAYER—

$\mathscr{H}$eavenly Father, I am imperfect, and I fail You in many ways. Thank You for Your forgiveness. When my students fall short of Your commandments, Lord, let me love them, let me correct them, and let me forgive them just as You have forgiven them…and me.

—*Amen*

++++++++++++++++++++++++++++++++++++++

OPTIMISM

++++++++++++++++++++++++++++++++++++++

The Lord is my light and my salvation; whom shall I fear? The Lord is the strength of my life; of whom shall I be afraid?

—Psalm 27:1 KJV

Make me to hear joy and gladness....

—Psalm 51:8 KJV

I can do everything through him that gives me strength.

—Philippians 4:13 NIV

Be of good courage, and he shall strengthen your heart, all ye that hope in the LORD.

—Psalm 31:24 KJV

Finally, brethren, whatsoever things are true, whatsoever things are honest, whatsoever things are just, whatsoever things are pure, whatsoever things are lovely, whatsoever things are of good report; if there be any virtue, and if there be any praise, think on these things.

—Philippians 4:8 KJV

We Christians have every reason to be optimistic about life. As John Calvin observed, "There is not one blade of grass, there is no color in this world that is not intended to make us rejoice." Today, think optimistically about yourself, your students, your school, and your world. And, share your optimism with everyone you meet and everyone you teach. You'll be better for it…and so will they.

Make the least of all that goes and the most of all that comes. Don't regret what is past. Cherish what you have. Look forward to all that is to come. And most important of all, rely moment by moment on Jesus Christ.

—Gigi Graham Tchividjian

—A Prayer—

Lord, let me be an expectant Christian. Let me expect the best from You, and let me look for the best in others. If I become discouraged, Father, turn my thoughts and my prayers to You. Let me trust You, Lord, to direct my life. And, let me be Your faithful, hopeful, optimistic teacher every day that I live.

—Amen

PATIENCE

We urge you, brethren, admonish the unruly, encourage the fainthearted, help the weak, be patient with everyone.

—1 Thessalonians 5:14 NASB

Be completely humble and gentle; be patient, bearing with one another in love.

—Ephesians 4:2 NIV

Wherefore seeing we also are compassed about with so great a cloud of witnesses, let us lay aside every weight, and the sin which doth so easily beset us, and let us run with patience the race that is set before us....

—Hebrews 12:1 KJV

Yet the LORD longs to be gracious to you; he rises to show you compassion. For the LORD is a God of justice. Blessed are all who wait for him!

—Isaiah 30:18 NIV

Wait on the LORD; Be of good courage, and He shall strengthen your heart; Wait, I say, on the LORD!

—Psalm 27:14 NKJV

Students, even the most dedicated and well-intentioned, are far from perfect. They make mistakes and misbehave; they don't always listen, and they don't always complete their assignments. In an imperfect school filled with imperfect people, a teacher's patience is tested many times each day. But, God's instructions are clear: "be patient, bearing with one another in love" (Ephesians 4:2 NIV). And, that's as it should be. After all, think how patient God has been with us.

When I am dealing with an all-powerful, all-knowing God, I, as a mere mortal, must offer my petitions not only with persistence, but also with patience. Someday I'll know why.

—*Ruth Bell Graham*

—A Prayer—

Heavenly Father, give me patience. Let me live according to Your plan and according to Your timetable. When I am hurried, slow me down. When I become impatient with my students, give me empathy. When I am frustrated by the demands of the day, give me peace. Today, let me be a patient teacher, Dear Lord, as I trust the Master Teacher for the Master Plan.

—*Amen*

PEACE

God has called us to live in peace.

—*1 Corinthians 7:15 NIV*

And let the peace of God rule in your hearts...and be ye thankful.

—*Colossians 3:15 KJV*

You will keep in perfect peace him whose mind is steadfast, because he trusts in you.

—*Isaiah 26:3 NIV*

I have told you these things, so that in me you may have peace. In this world you will have trouble. But take heart! I have overcome the world.

—*John 16:33 NIV*

The peace of God, which passeth all understanding, shall keep your hearts and minds through Christ Jesus.

—*Philippians 4:7 KJV*

*T*he beautiful words of John 14:27 give us hope: "Peace I leave with you, my peace I give unto you...." Jesus offers us peace, not as the world gives, but as He alone gives. We, as believers, can accept His peace or ignore it. Today, as a gift to yourself, to your family, and to your students, claim the inner peace that is your spiritual birthright: the peace of Jesus Christ. It is offered freely; it has been paid for in full; it is yours for the asking. So ask. And then share.

❧

The better acquainted you become with God, the less tension you feel and the more peace you possess.

—Charles Allen

—A Prayer—

*T*he peace that the world offers is fleeting, but You, Lord, offer a peace that is perfect and eternal. Let me turn the cares and burdens of my life over to You, Father, and let me feel the spiritual abundance that You offer through the person of Your Son, the Prince of Peace.

—Amen

PERSEVERANCE

Thanks be to God! He gives us the victory through our Lord Jesus Christ. Therefore, my dear brothers, stand firm. Let nothing move you. Always give yourselves fully to the work of the Lord, because you know that your labor in the Lord is not in vain.

—1 Corinthians 15:57-58 NIV

I do not consider myself yet to have taken hold of it. But one thing I do: Forgetting what is behind and straining toward what is ahead, I press on toward the goal to win the prize for which God has called me heavenward in Christ Jesus.

—Philippians 3:13-14 NIV

You need to persevere so that when you have done the will of God, you will receive what he has promised.

—Hebrews 10:36 NIV

I have fought a good fight, I have finished my course, I have kept the faith.

—2 Timothy 4:7 KJV

*T*his familiar saying is true: "Life is a marathon, not a sprint." And, the same can be said of the teaching profession. Teaching requires perseverance, especially on those difficult days when the students are in an uproar and the lesson plan is in disarray. But, our Savior, Christ Jesus, finished what He began, and so must we. Sometimes, God answers our prayers with silence, and when He does, we must patiently persevere. In times of trouble, we must seek God through prayer and lean upon His strength. Whatever our problems, He can handle them. Our job is to keep persevering until He does.

Never give in. Never give in. Never, never, never —in nothing great or small, large or petty—never give in except to conviction of honor and good sense.

—*Winston Churchill*

—A Prayer—

*H*eavenly Father, sometimes, this life is difficult indeed. Sometimes, we are burdened or fearful. Sometimes, we cry tears of bitterness or loss, but even then, You never leave our sides. Today, Lord, let me be a finisher of my faith. Let me persevere—even if the day is difficult— and let me follow Your Son Jesus Christ this day and forever.

—*Amen*

PRAISE

Praise the Lord, all nations! Extol him, all peoples! For great is his steadfast love toward us; and the faithfulness of the Lord endures forever. Praise the LORD!

—Psalm 117 RSV

I will praise the Lord at all times, I will constantly speak his praises.

—Psalm 34:1 NLT

Through Him then, let us continually offer up a sacrifice of praise to God, that is, the fruit of lips that give thanks to His name.

—Hebrews 13:15 NASB

Is anyone happy? Let him sing songs of praise.

—James 5:13 NIV

It is good to give thanks to the Lord, to sing praises to the Most High. It is good to proclaim your unfailing love in the morning, your faithfulness in the evening.

—Psalm 92:1-2 NLT

When is the best time to offer thanksgiving and praise to God? In church? At school? Before dinner is served? When we tuck little children into bed? None of the above. The best time to praise God is all day, every day, to the greatest extent we can, with thanksgiving in our hearts and with a song on our lips. Today, try to find a little more time to lift your thankful heart to God in prayer. You owe Him everything, including your praise.

The Creator loves you very much since He gives you so many good things. Therefore, be careful not to be ungrateful, but strive always to praise God.

—*Saint Francis of Assisi*

—A Prayer—

Father, Your hand created the smallest grain of sand and the grandest stars in the heavens. You watch over Your entire creation, and You watch over me. Thank You, Lord, for loving this world so much that You sent Your Son to die for our sins. Let me always be grateful for the priceless gift of Your Son, and let me praise Your holy name forever.

—*Amen*

PRAYER

Rejoice evermore. Pray without ceasing. In every thing give thanks: for this is the will of God in Christ Jesus concerning you.

—1 Thessalonians 5:16-18 KJV

The effective prayer of a righteous man can accomplish much.

—James 5:16 NASB

Whatever you ask for in prayer, believe that you have received it, and it will be yours.

—Mark 11:24 NIV

I sought the LORD, and he heard me, and delivered me from all my fears.

—Psalm 34:4 KJV

Ask and it shall be given to you; seek and you shall find; knock and it shall be opened to you. For every one who asks receives, and he who seeks finds, and to him who knocks it shall be opened.

—Matthew 7:7-8 NASB

*P*rayer changes things and it changes us. Today, instead of turning things over in your mind, turn them over to God in prayer. Instead of worrying about your next decision, decide to let God lead the way. Don't limit your prayers to meals or to bedtime. Pray constantly about things great and small. God is listening, and He wants to hear from you. Now.

If the spiritual life is to be healthy and under the full power of the Holy Spirit, praying without ceasing will be natural.

—Andrew Murray

—A Prayer—

I pray to You, Heavenly Father, because You desire it and because I need it. Prayer not only changes things, it changes me. Help me, Lord, never to face the demands of the day without first spending time with You.

—Amen

RESPONSIBILITY

Even a child is known by his actions, by whether his conduct is pure and right.

—Proverbs 20:11 NIV

Thus you will walk in the ways of good men and keep to the paths of the righteous. For the upright will live in the land, and the blameless will remain in it; but the wicked will be cut off from the land, and the unfaithful will be torn from it.

—Proverbs 2:20-22 NIV

And you shall do what is good and right in the sight of the Lord, that it may be well with you....

—Deuteronomy 6:18 NASB

I the Lord search the heart and examine the mind, to reward a man according to his conduct, according to what his deeds deserve.

—Jeremiah 17:10 NIV

Light shines on the godly, and joy on those who do right. May all who are godly be happy in the Lord and praise his holy name.

—Psalm 97:11-12 NLT

As teachers, we find ourselves preaching the gospel of responsible behavior. Unfortunately, our sermons often fall upon deaf ears. Despite warnings to the contrary, young people sometimes behave inappropriately; they sometimes behave impulsively; they sometimes behave foolishly. Why? Because they are human beings and because they are young. Our task, as adults, is to never give up, but instead to keep teaching the wisdom of responsible behavior by word and by example. And the greatest of these, of course, is example.

Action springs not from thought, but from a readiness for responsibility.

—*Dietrich Bonhoeffer*

—A Prayer—

Lord, it is so much easier to speak of the righteous life than it is to live it. Let me live responsibly, and let my actions be consistent with my beliefs. May every step that I take reflect Your truth and Your love, and may I live a life that is worthy of Your love and Your grace.

—*Amen*

RIGHTEOUSNESS

For the eyes of the Lord are over the righteous, and his ears are open unto their prayers: but the face of the Lord is against them that do evil.

—*1 Peter 3:12 KJV*

Blessed are the pure of heart, for they will see God.

—*Matthew 5:8 NIV*

But seek first his kingdom and his righteousness, and all these things will be given to you as well.

—*Matthew 6:33 NIV*

The Lord will not reject his people; he will not abandon his own special possession. Judgement will come again for the righteous, and those who are upright will have a reward.

—*Psalm 94:14-15 NLT*

The righteous shall flourish like the palm tree: he shall grow like a cedar in Lebanon.

—*Psalm 92:12 KJV*

The author of the Christian classic *My Utmost For His Highest*, Oswald Chambers, advised, "Never support an experience which does not have God as its source, and faith in God as its result." These words serve as a powerful reminder that, as Christians, we are called to walk with God and obey His Word. But, we live in a world that presents countless temptations for adults and even more temptations for young people. When confronted with sin, we have clear instructions: walk—or better yet—run in the opposite direction. When we do, we reap the blessings that God has promised to all those who live according to His Will.

We must appropriate the tender mercy of God every day after conversion, or problems quickly develop. We need his grace daily in order to live a righteous life.

—Jim Cymbala

—A Prayer—

Lord, when I turn my thoughts away from You and Your Word, I suffer. But when I trust in Your commandments, when I turn my thoughts, my faith, and my prayers to You, I am safe. Direct my path far from the temptations and distractions of the world. Let me discover Your will and follow it, Father, this day and always.

Amen

SEEKING GOD

Let the hearts of those who seek the Lord rejoice. Look to the Lord and his strength; seek his face always.

—1 Chronicles 16:10-11 NIV

If my people, which are called by my name, shall humble themselves, and pray, and seek my face, and turn from their wicked ways; then will I hear from heaven, and will forgive their sin, and will heal their land.

—1 Chronicles 7:14 KJV

Anyone who comes to him [God] must believe that he exists and that he rewards those who earnestly seek him.

—Hebrews 11:6 NIV

You will seek me and find me when you seek me with all your heart.

—Jeremiah 29:13 NIV

Sow for yourselves righteousness, reap the fruit of unfailing love, and break up your unplowed ground; for it is time to seek the LORD, until he comes and showers righteousness on you.

—Hosea 10:12 NIV

Sometimes, in the hustle of our daily duties, God seems far away. But He is not. God is everywhere you have ever been and everywhere you will ever go. He is with you night and day; He knows your every thought; He hears your every heartbeat. He is with you at home, and He is with you in the classroom. When you earnestly seek Him, you will find Him because He is here, waiting patiently for you to reach out to Him...right here...right now.

Life's major pursuit is not knowing self, but knowing God. Unless God is the major pursuit of our lives, all other pursuits are dead-end streets, including trying to know ourselves.

—*Chuck Swindoll*

—A PRAYER—

How comforting it is, Dear Lord, to know that if I seek You, I will find You. You are with me, Father, every step that I take. Let me reach out to You, and let me praise You for revealing Your Word, Your way, and Your love.

—*Amen*

SERVING GOD

So then, men ought to regard us as servants of Christ and as those entrusted with the secret things of God. Now it is required that those who have been given a trust must prove faithful.

—1 Corinthians 4:1-2 NIV

And now, O Israel, what does the LORD your God ask of you but to fear the LORD your God, to walk in all his ways, to love him, to serve the LORD your God with all your heart and with all your soul....

—Deuteronomy 10:12 NIV

Make a joyful noise unto the LORD, all ye lands. Serve the LORD with gladness: come before his presence with singing.

—Psalm 100:1-2 KJV

Therefore, I urge you, brothers, in view of God's mercy, to offer your bodies as living sacrifices, holy and pleasing to God—this is your spiritual act of worship.

—Romans 12:1 NIV

How can we serve God? By sharing His message, His mercy, and His love with those who cross our paths. Everywhere we look, it seems, the needs are great, and at every turn, or so it seems, so are the temptations. But, our challenge is clear: we must love God, obey His commandments, trust His Son, and serve His children. When we place the Lord in His rightful place—at the center of our lives—then we claim spiritual treasures that will endure forever.

God wants us to serve Him with a willing spirit, one that would choose no other way.

—*Beth Moore*

—A Prayer—

Lord, I can serve only one master; let me serve You. Let my actions be pleasing to You; let my words reflect Your infinite love; let my prayers be sincere and my thoughts be pure. In everything that I do, Father, let me praise You and serve You today and for eternity.

—*Amen*

SERVING OTHERS

But whosoever will be great among you, let him be your minister; and whosoever will be chief among you, let him be your servant: even as the Son of man came not to be ministered unto, but to minister, and to give his life a ransom for many.

—Matthew 20:26-28 KJV

The greatest among you will be your servant. For whoever exalts himself will be humbled, and whoever humbles himself will be exalted.

—Matthew 23:11 NIV

Each of you should look not only to your own interests, but also to the interest of others.

—Philippians 2:4 NIV

A generous man will prosper; he who refreshes others will himself be refreshed.

—Proverbs 11:25 NIV

The one who blesses others is abundantly blessed; those who help others are helped.

—Proverbs 11:25 MSG

*T*he teachings of Jesus are clear: We will achieve greatness through service to others. And, as teachers, we have unique and important opportunities for service. Each time we pause to help a student, each time we offer a kind word or a pat on the back, we have done so in accordance with the commandments of our Savior. If we seek spiritual greatness, we must first become servants. Then, and only then, will we achieve greatness in the eyes of our Lord.

Employ whatever God has entrusted you with, in doing good, all possible good, in every possible kind and degree.

—John Wesley

—A Prayer—

*F*ather in heaven…when Jesus humbled Himself and became a servant, He also became an example for His followers. Today, as I serve my students, I do so in the name of Jesus, my Lord and Master. Guide my steps, Father, and let my service be pleasing to You.

—Amen

STRENGTH

Those who hope in the LORD will renew their strength. They will soar on wings like eagles; they will run and not grow weary, they will walk and not be faint.

—Isaiah 40:31 NIV

He said unto me, My grace is sufficient for thee: for my strength is made perfect in weakness.

—2 Corinthians 12:9 KJV

Whatever your hand finds to do, do it with all your might....

—Ecclesiastes 9:10 NIV

The LORD is my strength and my song....

—Exodus 15:2 NIV

I can do all things through Him who strengthens me.

—Philippians 4:13 NASB

Where can we turn when the demands of the day leave us exhausted? We can turn to God for comfort and renewal. God is a never-ending source of strength and courage for those who call upon Him. When we are weary, He gives us strength. When we see no hope, God reminds us of His promises. When we grieve, God wipes away our tears. Whatever our circumstances, God will protect us and care for us…if we let Him.

Worry does not empty tomorrow of its sorrow; it empties today of its strength.

—*Corrie ten Boom*

—A PRAYER—

Heavenly Father, You are my strength and my protector. When I am troubled, You comfort me. When I am discouraged, You lift me up. When I am afraid, You deliver me. Let me turn to You, Lord, when I am weak. In times of adversity, let me trust Your plan, Lord, and whatever my circumstances, let me look to You for my strength and my salvation.

—*Amen*

TALENTS

Each man has his own gift from God; one has this gift, another has that.

—*1 Corinthians 7:7 NIV*

The man who had received the five talents brought the other five. "Master," he said, "you entrusted me with five talents. See, I have gained five more." His master replied, "Well done, good and faithful servant! You have been faithful with a few things; I will put you in charge of many things. Come and share your master's happiness."

—*Matthew 25:20-21 NIV*

I remind you to fan into flame the gift of God.

—*2 Timothy 1:6 NIV*

Thanks be to God for his indescribable gift!

—*2 Corinthians 9:15 NIV*

*T*he old saying is both familiar and true: "What we are is God's gift to us; what we become is our gift to God." Each of us, teachers and students alike, possesses special talents, gifted by God, that can be nurtured carefully or ignored totally. Our challenge is to make the most of our own God-given talents and to encourage our students to do likewise.

One thing taught large in the Holy Scriptures is that while God gives His gifts freely, He will require a strict accounting of them at the end of the road. Each man is personally responsible for his store, be it large or small, and will be required to explain his use of it before the judgment seat of Christ.

—A. W. Tozer

—A Prayer—

*L*ord, You have blessed me with a love that is far beyond my limited understanding. You loved me before I was ever born; You sent Your Son Jesus to redeem me from my sins; You have given me the gift of eternal life. And, You have given me special talents; let me use those talents to the best of my ability and to the glory of Your kingdom so that I might be a good and faithful teacher this day and forever.

—Amen

TEACHING

A wise man's heart guides his mouth, and his lips promote instruction.

—Proverbs 16:23 NIV

Whoever gives heed to instruction prospers, and blessed is he that trusts in the Lord.

—Proverbs 16:20 NIV

A wise person gets known for insight; gracious words add to one's reputation. True intelligence is a spring of fresh water, while fools sweat it out the hard way.

—Proverbs 16:21-22 MSG

Simpletons only learn the hard way, but the wise learn by listening.

—Proverbs 21:11 MSG

It takes wisdom to build a house, and understanding to set it on a firm foundation; it takes knowledge to furnish its rooms with fine furniture and beautiful draperies.

—Proverbs 24:3-4 MSG

$\mathcal{D}$aniel Webster once wrote, "If we work in marble, it will perish; if we work upon brass, time will efface it; if we rear temples, they will crumble into dust; but if we work upon immortal minds and instill in them just principles, we are then engraving upon tablets which no time will efface, but which will brighten and brighten to all eternity." These words remind us of the glorious opportunities that are available to those of us who teach. May we, with God's help, touch the hearts and minds of our students and, in doing so, refashion this wonderful world...and the next.

The object of teaching a child is to enable him to get along without his teacher.

—*Elbert Hubbard*

—A PRAYER—

$\mathcal{Y}$ou have warned, Lord, of the awesome responsibility of being a teacher. I am an instructor to my students. As they listen and observe my teachings, Father, may they see You in all I say and do.

—*Amen*

THANKSGIVING

Oh my soul, bless GOD, don't forget a single blessing!

—Psalm 103:2 MSG

O come, let us sing unto the LORD: let us make a joyful noise to the rock of our salvation. Let us come before his presence with thanksgiving, and make a joyful noise unto him with psalms.

—Psalm 95:1-2 KJV

I know that the righteous personally thank you, that good people are secure in your presence.

—Psalm 140:13 MSG

Do you see what we've got? An unshakable kingdom! And do you see how thankful we must be? Not only thankful, but brimming with worship, deeply reverent before God.

—Hebrews 12:27-28 MSG

As believing Christians, we are blessed beyond measure. And, as teachers, we are especially blessed by the opportunity to educate young minds and shape young lives. Thanksgiving should become a habit, a regular part of our daily routines. God has blessed us beyond measure, and we owe Him everything, including our eternal praise. To paraphrase the familiar children's blessing, "God is great, God is good, let us thank Him for…everything!"

A child of God should be a visible beatitude for joy and a living doxology for gratitude.

—*C. H. Spurgeon*

—A Prayer—

Heavenly Father, Your gifts are greater than I can imagine. May I live each day with thanksgiving in my heart and praise on my lips. Thank You for the gift of Your Son and for the promise of eternal life. Let me share the joyous news of Jesus Christ, and let my life be a testimony to His love and His grace.

—*Amen*

TODAY

This is the day the LORD has made; let us rejoice and be glad in it.

—Psalm 118:24 NIV

Encourage one another daily, as long as it is Today....

—Hebrews 3:13 NIV

Give your entire attention to what God is doing right now, and don't get worked up about what may or may not happen tomorrow. God will help you deal with whatever hard things come up when the time comes.

—Matthew 6:33-34 MSG

For he says, "In the time of my favor I heard you, and in the day of salvation I helped you." I tell you, now is the time of God's favor, now is the day of salvation.

—2 Corinthians 6:2 NIV

The words of Psalm 118:24 remind us of a profound yet simple truth: "This is the day which the LORD hath made; we will rejoice and be glad in it" (KJV). For Christian believers, every day begins and ends with God and His Son. We give thanks to Him when we treasure each day and use it to the fullest. Today, may we give thanks for this day and for the One who created it…and may we encourage our students to do likewise.

It has been well said that no man ever sank under the burden of the day. It is when tomorrow's burden is added to the burden of today that the weight is more than a man can bear. Never load yourselves so, my friends. If you find yourselves so loaded, at least remember this: it is your own do-ing, not God's. He begs you to leave the future to Him and mind the present.

—George MacDonald

—A Prayer—

Heavenly Father, this is the day that You have given me. Let me use it, Lord, according to Your master plan, and let me give thanks for Your blessings. Enable me to live each moment to the fullest, totally involved in Your will.

—Amen

TRUSTING GOD

For the Lord God is our light and our protector. He gives us grace and glory. No good thing will the Lord withhold from those who do what is right. O Lord Almighty, happy are those who trust in you.

—Psalm 84:11-12 NLT

Trust ye in the LORD for ever: for in the LORD JEHOVAH is everlasting strength.

—Isaiah 26:4 KJV

We...worship by the Spirit of God...glory in Christ Jesus, and...put no confidence in the flesh.

—Philippians 3:3 NIV

Do not let your hearts be troubled. Trust in God; trust also in me. In my Father's house are many rooms; if it were not so, I would have told you. I am going there to prepare a place for you.

—John 14:1-2 NIV

The LORD is my rock, and my fortress, and my deliverer; my God, my strength, in whom I will trust....

—Psalm 18:2 KJV

Are you tired? Discouraged? Fearful? Be comforted and trust God. Are you worried or anxious? Be confident in God's power. He will never desert you. Do you see no hope for the future? Be courageous and call upon God. He will protect you and then use you according to His purposes. Are you grieving? Know that God hears your suffering. He will comfort you and, in time, He will dry your tears. Are you confused? Listen to the quiet voice of your Heavenly Father. He is not a God of confusion. Talk with Him; listen to Him; trust Him. He is steadfast, and He is your Protector...forever.

Persons of true character are neither optimists nor pessimists, but realists who have confidence in God.

—*Warren Wiersbe*

—A Prayer—

Dear Lord, when I trust in things of this earth, I will be disappointed. But, when I put my faith in You, I am secure. You are my rock and my shield. Upon Your firm foundation I will build my life. When I am worried, Lord, let me trust in You. You will love me and protect me, and You will share Your boundless grace today, tomorrow, and forever.

—*Amen*

WISDOM

Do not deceive yourselves. If any one of you thinks he is wise by the standards of this age, he should become a "fool" so that he may become wise. For the wisdom of this world is foolishness in God's sight.

—1 Corinthians 3:18-19 NIV

But if any of you lacks wisdom, let him ask of God, who gives to all generously and without reproach, and it will be given to him.

—James 1:5 NASB

The wisdom that is from above is first pure, then peaceable, gentle, and easy to be entreated, full of mercy and good fruits, without partiality, and without hypocrisy.

—James 3:17 KJV

Reverence for the Lord is the foundation of true wisdom. The rewards of wisdom come to all who obey him.

—Psalm 111:10 NLT

Wisdom is not accumulated overnight. It is like a savings account that accrues slowly over time, and the person who consistently adds to his account will eventually accumulate a great sum. The secret to success is consistency. Do you seek wisdom for yourself and for your students? Then keep learning and keep motivating them to do likewise. The ultimate source of wisdom, of course, is—first and foremost—the Word of God. When you begin a daily study of God's Word and live according to His commandments, you will become wise...and so, in time, will your students.

The fruit of wisdom is Christlikeness, peace, humility, and love. And, the root of it is faith in Christ as the manifested wisdom of God.

—*J. I. Packer*

—A PRAYER—

God, just as Solomon asked for wisdom to rule Judea, I ask for wisdom to teach my students. Make me wise in Your ways and in Your Holy Word so that those I teach might grow and mature each day in the center of Your will.

—*Amen*

WORDS

To everything there is a season…a time to keep silence, and a time to speak.

—Ecclesiastes 3:1,7 KJV

For out of the overflow of the heart the mouth speaks.

—Matthew 12:34 NIV

But I say unto you, That every idle word that men shall speak, they shall give account thereof in the day of judgment. For by thy words thou shalt be justified, and by thy words thou shalt be condemned.

—Matthew 12:36-37 KJV

Reckless words pierce like a sword, but the tongue of the wise brings healing.

—Proverbs 12:18 NIV

Let the words of my mouth, and the meditations of my heart, be acceptable in thy sight, O Lord, my strength and my redeemer.

—Psalm 19:14 KJV

*T*hink...pause...then speak: How wise is the teacher who can communicate in this fashion. But, all too often, in the rush to have our messages heard, we speak first and think later...with unfortunate results. Today, make the resolution to encourage all who cross your path, especially your students. Measure your words carefully. Speak wisely, not impulsively. Your words will offer encouragement and hope to a classroom—and to a world—that needs both.

Kind words can be short and easy to speak, but their echoes are endless.

—Mother Teresa

—A PRAYER—

*L*ord, You have warned me that I will be judged by the words I speak. And, You have commanded me to choose my words carefully so that I might be a source of encouragement and hope to my students. Keep me mindful, Lord, that I have influence on many people...make me an influence for good. And may the words that I speak today be worthy of the One who has saved me forever.

—Amen

WORK

Be strong and courageous, and do the work. Do not be afraid or discouraged, for the Lord God, my God, is with you.

—1 Chronicles 28:20 NIV

But as for you, be strong and do not give up, for your work will be rewarded.

—2 Chronicles 15:7 NIV

Now this I say, he who sows sparingly will also reap sparingly, and he who sows bountifully will also reap bountifully.

—2 Corinthians 9:6 NASB

Whatever you do, work at it with all your heart, as working for the Lord, not for men.

—Colossians 3:23 NIV

Don't work hard only when your master is watching and then shirk when he isn't looking; work hard and with gladness all the time, as though working for Christ, doing the will of God with all your hearts.

—Ephesians 6:6-7 TLB

*B*eing a teacher is not an easy job. The demands and pressures of the classroom, combined with late-night paper-grading marathons and lesson preparations, can leave even the most experienced teacher feeling overworked and under appreciated. Thankfully, teaching is not only a difficult job, it is also a highly rewarding one. Reaching for great things usually requires work and lots of it, which is perfectly fine with God. After all, He knows that you're up to the task, and He has big plans for you and for your students. Very big plans...

❧

I long to accomplish a great and noble task, but it is my chief duty to accomplish small tasks as if they were great and noble.

—*Helen Keller*

—A Prayer—

*L*ord, I know that You desire a bountiful harvest for all Your children. But, You have instructed us that we must sow before we reap, not after. Help me, Lord, to sow the seeds of Your abundance everywhere I go. Let me be diligent in all my teaching and give me patience to wait for Your harvest. In time, Lord, let me reap the harvest that is found in Your will for my life.

—*Amen*

WORRY

Peace I leave with you, my peace I give unto you: not as the world giveth, give I unto you. Let not your heart be troubled, neither let it be afraid.

—*John 14:27 KJV*

Therefore do not worry about tomorrow, for tomorrow will worry about itself. Each day has enough trouble of its own.

—*Matthew 6:34 NIV*

Therefore I tell you, do not worry about your life, what you will eat or drink; or about your body, what you will wear. Is life not more important than food and the body more important than clothes? Look at the birds of the air; they do not sow or reap or store away in barns, and yet your heavenly Father feeds them. Are you not much more valuable than they? Who of you by worrying can add a single hour to his life?

—*Matthew 6:25-27 NIV*

Come to me, all you who are weary and burdened, and I will give you rest. Take my yoke upon you and learn from me, for I am gentle and humble in heart, and you will find rest for your souls. For my yoke is easy and my burden is light.

—*Matthew 11:28-30 NIV*

*E*ven though we, as Christians, have the assurance of salvation—and the promise of God's love and protection—we find ourselves fretting over the countless details of our lives. Jesus understood our concerns when He spoke the reassuring words we can read in the 6th chapter of Matthew. This beautiful passage reminds us that God still sits in His heaven and we are His beloved children. So, perhaps, we should worry less and trust God a lot more, and that's as it should be because He is trustworthy…and we are protected.

Because God is my sovereign Lord, I was not worried. He manages perfectly, day and night, year in and year out, the movements of the stars, the staggering coordination of events that goes on at the molecular level in order to hold things together. There is no doubt that he can manage the timing of my days and weeks.

—*Elisabeth Elliot*

—A Prayer—

*L*ord, You sent Your Son to live as a man on this earth, and You know what it means to be human. You understand my worries and fears, Lord, and You forgive me when I am weak. When my faith begins to wane, help me, Lord, to trust You more.

—*Amen*

WORSHIP

But the hour cometh, and now is, when the true worshippers shall worship the Father in spirit and in truth: for the Father seeketh such to worship him.

—John 4:23 KJV

Then saith Jesus unto him, Get thee hence, Satan: for it is written, Thou shalt worship the Lord thy God, and him only shalt thou serve.

—Matthew 4:10 KJV

Blessed are they which do hunger and thirst after righteousness: for they shall be filled.

—Matthew 5:6 KJV

Worship the Lord with gladness. Come before him, singing with joy. Acknowledge that the Lord is God! He made us, and we are his. We are his people, the sheep of his pasture.

—Psalm 100:2-3 NLT

Happy are those who hear the joyful call to worship, for they will walk in the light of your presence, Lord.

—Psalm 89:15 NLT

Some people choose to worship God and, as a result, reap the joy that He intends for His children. Others distance themselves from God by worshiping such things as earthly possessions or personal gratification. When they do so, they suffer. Today, make every aspect of your life a cause for celebration and worship. Praise God for the blessings and opportunities that He has given you, and live according to the beautiful words found in the 5th chapter of 1 Thessalonians: "Rejoice evermore. Pray without ceasing. In every thing give thanks: for this is the will of God in Christ Jesus concerning you" (16-18).

∝

In Biblical worship you do not find the repetition of a phrase; instead, you find the worshipers rehearsing the character of God and His ways, reminding Him of His faithfulness and His wonderful promises.

—*Kay Arthur*

—A Prayer—

This world is a place of distractions and temptations. But when I worship You, Father, You set my path—and my heart—straight. Whether I am in Your house or going about my daily teaching activities, let me worship You, not only with words and deeds, but also with my heart.

—*Amen*

Delight thyself also in the LORD;
and he shall give thee the desires
of thine heart.

—

Psalm 37:4 KJV